The Mother's Quotation Book

A Literary Companion

Edited by

Elspeth McIntosh

ROBERT HALE · LONDON

ISBN 0 7090 5427 0

Robert Hale Limited
Clerkenwell House
Clerkenwell Green
London EC1R 0HT

2   4   6   8   10   9   7   5   3   1

Photoset in Goudy by
Derek Doyle & Associates, Mold, Clwyd.
Printed and bound in Great Britain by
WBC Book Manufacturers

THE MOTHER'S
QUOTATION BOOK

Preface

As I was putting the finishing touches to this collection of quotations, my friend with whom I was staying in the country pointed out a duck with her ducklings who lived beside the nearby pond.

Originally, there had been seven ducklings, but as we watched on that summer's day, we could see only three; such is nature's way, when left to itself. But despite the threats from predatory animals all around, the mother duck continued to patrol the pond, hurrying any of the three remaining ducklings if they dawdled on their own for too long, and leading them to gather up the bread crumbs that we threw to them.

Oh brave mother duck! I thought to myself, and was reminded of many of the quotations in this book, which either celebrate or take for granted the stoicism of women who are responsible for their children. Mothers are often presented either as figures of praise or as figures to be wary of, but either way their protective role is always taken for granted.

And perhaps unsurprisingly, many men quoted in this volume sail perilously close to sentimentality when recalling their own mothers. Lacretelle says, 'I would desire for a friend the son who never resisted the tears of his mother,' while Kipling's views are, I would suspect, often a little mawkish for many women's tastes.

Finally, motherhood as displayed in many of these quotations is often used as a metaphor for creation in many fields, and I hope that readers will find the contrast between the metaphorical and the practical in some of the entries enlightening.

I would like to dedicate this volume to all mothers – ducks and all! – who have experienced some of the sentiments in this book, and may perhaps recognize others with a wry smile. If it serves any purpose at all, it will at least show that, for mothers, there is nothing new under the sun!

Acknowledgements

Acknowledgments are due to the following for permission to quote from works in copyright: *At Mrs Lippincote's* by Elizabeth Taylor, Virago Press; *The Outsider* by Albert Camus, translated by Joseph Laredo, Hamish Hamilton Ltd; *Cider With Rosie* by Laurie Lee, Chatto and Windus; quotations from the works of George Bernard Shaw, the Society of Authors on behalf of the Bernard Shaw Estate; *Writer's Notebook* by W. Somerset Maugham, William Heinemann Ltd; permission has been sought for all quotations still in copyright, but any omissions at this stage will be rectified in future editions.

Socrates, when condemned, philosophised with his disciples; a mother, on the point of undergoing a similar fate, may discourse with her children.

JOSEPHINE (1763–1814)
in *Lives of Celebrated Women* by Samuel Griswold Goodrich
1844

Years to a mother bring distress
But do not make her love the less.
WILLIAM WORDSWORTH (1770–1850)
The Affliction of Margaret

First and foremost I should wish a woman I loved to be a mother ... From the first I would impress on her the holiness of motherhood ... But for the sake of that very motherhood I would teach her that she must be an intellectual being – that without a strong deliberate mind she is only capable of the animal office of bearing children, not of rearing them. It pains me to see a fine intelligent girl, directly she marries, putting aside intellectual things as no longer pertinent to her daily life.

BEATRICE WEBB (1858–1943)
Diary

9

Womanliness means only motherhood;
All love begins and ends there.
ROBERT BROWNING (1812–89)
Inn Album

He that would the daughter win
Must with the mother first begin.
JOHN RAY (1627–1705)
A Collection of English Proverbs
1670

Where yet was ever found a mother,
Who'd give her booby for another?
JOHN GAY (*c.* 1685–1732)
Fables: The Mother, the Nurse and the Fairy

Goslings would lead their mother to pasture.
OUDIN
1640

God pardons like a mother who kisses the offence into
everlasting forgetfulness.
HENRY WARD BEECHER (1813–87)
Proverbs from a Plymouth Pulpit

O Mrs. Higden, Mrs. Higden, you was a woman and a mother, and a mangler in a million million.
CHARLES DICKENS (1812–70)
Our Mutual Friend

Thy nightly visits to my chamber made,
That thou mightst know me safe and warmly laid;
Thy morning bounties ere I left my home,
The biscuit, or confectionary plum;
The fragrant waters on my cheek bestowed
By thy own hand, till fresh they shone and glow'd:
All this, and more endearing still than all,
Thy constant flow of love, that knew no fall,
Ne'er roughened by those cataracts and brakes,
That humour interposed too often makes.
WILLIAM COWPER (1731–1800)
On the Receipt of My Mother's Picture Out of Norfolk
from *Poems*, 1798

As is the mother, so is her daughter.
EZEKIEL 16:44

When Eve was brought unto Adam, he became filled with the Holy Spirit and gave her the most sanctified, the most glorious of appelations. He called her Eva, that is to say, the Mother of All. He did not style her wife, but simply mother – mother of all living creatures. In this consists the glory and the most precious ornament of woman.

MARTIN LUTHER (1483–1546)

The good mother says, not, Will you? but gives.

GEORGE HERBERT (1593–1633)
Outlandish Proverbs
1640

A wise son maketh a glad father: but a foolish son is the heaviness of his mother.

PSALMS 10:1

Every one can keep house better than her mother till she trieth.

T. FULLER (1608–61)
Gnomologia: Adagies and Proverbs
1732

That scoundrel, sir! Why, he'd sharpen a knife upon his father's tombstone to kill his mother.

DOUGLAS WILLIAM JERROLD (1803–57)
Wit and Opinions of Douglas William Jerrold
1858

My mother's general principles of first treatment were, to guard me with steady watchfulness from all avoidable pain or danger; and, for the rest, to let me amuse myself as I liked, provided I was neither fretful nor troublesome. But the law was, that I should find my own amusement. No toys of any kind were at first allowed ... On one of my birthdays, thinking to overcome my mother's resolution by splendour of temptation, [my Croydon aunt] bought the most radiant Punch and Judy she could find in all the Soho bazaar ... My mother was obliged to accept them; but afterwards quietly told me it was not right that I should have them; and I never saw them again.

JOHN RUSKIN (1819–1900)
Praeterita
1885–99

A light-hearted mother makes a heavy-heeled daughter.

JOHN RAY (1627–1705)
A Collection of English Proverbs
1670

If snow falls on the far field
Where travellers
Spend the night,
I ask you cranes,
To warm my child in your wings.
> ANON (c. 733)
> *Mother's Song*
> translated by Willis Barnstone
> in *A Book of Women Poets*
> edited by Aliki Barnstone and Willis Barnstone

Love still has something of the sea
From whence his mother rose.
> SIR CHARLES SEDLEY (1639–1701)
> *Love Still Has Something*

Just before the battle, Mother,
I am thinking most of you,
While upon the field we're watching
With the enemy in view.
> GEORGE F. ROOT
> *Song*
> 1855

Like mother, like daughter.
> 16TH CENTURY PROVERB

O mother, mother, make my bed,
O make it soft and narrow:
My love has died for me to-day,
I'll die for him tomorrow.
    ANON
    The Ballad of Barbara Allen's Cruelty

A child may have too much of his mother's blessing.
    J. CLARKE
    Paroemiologia Anglo-Latina
    1639

Mighty is the force of motherhood! It transforms all things by its vital heat; it turns timidity into fierce courage, and dreadless defiance into tremulous submission; it turns thoughtlessness into foresight, and yet stills all anxiety into calm content; it makes selfishness become self-denial, and gives even to hard vanity the glance of admiring love.
    GEORGE ELIOT (1819–80)
    The Mill on the Floss
    1860

An ounce of mother-wit is worth a pound of clergy.
    17TH CENTURY PROVERB

The evil hearted Grocer
Would call his mother 'Ma'am',
And bow at her and bob at her,
Her aged soul to damn.

> G. K. CHESTERTON (1874–1936)
> *Song Against Grocers*

Mother Mother shave me
let us go and see the bird
with the bright red beak.
Let's go to the bush Mother
to the small bush.
Let's brush off our hair
each other's hair.
Let us leave a guide-bone
for the goats that graze
that graze in my little field.
The little field I cultivate
I cultivate with a hoe
I bought in the European's home
the home where moss grows.
We shall bring forth a child
and we shall name him
and we shall name him *darkness.*

> TRADITIONAL NYASA POEM
> translated by Ulli Beier
> in *African Poetry: An Anthology of Traditional*
>   *African Poetry*

19

So for the mother's sake the child was dear,
And dearer was the mother for the child.
SAMUEL TAYLOR COLERIDGE (1772–1834)
*Sonnet to a Friend Who Asked How I Felt When
the Nurse First Presented My Infant to Me*

The mother is a matchless beast.
KELLY
Proverb

A mother's love is indeed the golden link that binds
youth to age; and he is still but a child, however time
may have furrowed his cheek, or silvered his brow,
who can yet recall, with a softened heart, the fond
devotion, or the gentle chidings, of the best friend
that God ever gives us.
CHRISTIAN NESTELL BOVEE

Don't let's go to the dogs tonight,
For mother will be there.
A.P. HERBERT (1890–1971)
She-Shanties: 'Don't Let's Go to the Dogs
1926

O hush thee, my babie, thy sire was a knight,
Thy mother a lady, both lovely and bright.
    SIR WALTER SCOTT (1771–1832)
    Lullaby of an Indian Chief

Father, Mother, and Me,
Sister and Auntie say
All the people like us are We,
And everyone else is They.
    RUDYARD KIPLING (1865–1936)
    We and They

CHILD	O Mother, lay your hand on my brow!
	O mother, mother, where am I now?
	Why is the room so gaunt and great?
	Why am I lying awake so late?
MOTHER	Fear not at all: the night is still.
	Nothing is here that means you ill.
	Nothing but lamps the whole town through,
	And never a child awake but you.
CHILD	Mother, mother, speak low in my ear,
	Some of the things are so great and near,
	Some are so small and far away,
	I have a fear that I cannot say.

21

What have I done, and what do I
    fear,
And why are you crying, mother dear?
MOTHER   Out in the city, sounds begin.
Thank the kind God, the carts come in!
An hour or two more, and God is so
    kind,
The day shall be blue in the window
    blind,
Then shall my child go sweetly asleep,
And dream of the birds and the hills of
    sheep.

ROBERT LOUIS STEVENSON (1850–94)
The Sick Child
from *Underwoods*, 1887

When the coster's finished jumping on his mother
He loves to lie a-basking in the sun.

W. S. GILBERT (1836–1911)
The Pirates of Penzance
1879

Happy he
With such a mother! faith in womankind
Beats with his blood, and trust in all things high

Comes easy to him, and tho' he trip and fall
He shall not blind his soul with clay.
ALFRED, LORD TENNYSON (1809–92)
The Princess

Little Polly Flinders
Sat among the cinders,
Warming her pretty little toes.
Her mother came and caught her,
And whipped her little daughter
For spoiling her nice new clothes.
ORIGINAL DITTIES FOR THE NURSERY
1805

Dance, little baby, dance up high,
Never mind, baby, mother is nigh.
ANN TAYLOR (1782–1866)
Rhymes for the Nursery
1806

Ah, my little son, thou hast murdered thy mother!
And therefore I suppose thou that art a murderer so
young, thou art full likely to be a manly man in thine
age … when he is christened let call him Tristram,
that is as much to say as a sorrowful birth.
SIR THOMAS MALORY (*fl.* 1470)
Le Morte D'Arthur

I miss thee, my Mother, when young health has
    fled,
And I sink in the languor of pain.
Where, where is the arm that once pillowed my
    head,
And the ear that once heard me complain?
Other hands may support me, gentle accents may
    fall –
For the fond and the true are still mine:
I've a blessing for each; I am grateful to all
But whose care can be as soothing as thine?

    ELIZA COOK (1818–89)
    Poems
    1870

What are Raphael's Madonnas, but the shadow of a
mother's love, fixed in permanent outline forever?

    THOMAS WENTWORTH HIGGINSON (1823–1911)

Honour thy Father and thy Mother; that thy days may
be long upon the land which the Lord thy God giveth
thee.

    THE FIFTH COMMANDMENT
    The Book of Common Prayer

All that I am my mother made me.
> JOHN QUINCEY ADAMS (1767–1848)
> US President

What the mother sings to the cradle goes all the way down to the grave.
> HENRY WARD BEECHER (1813–87)
> *Proverbs From a Plymouth Pulpit*

Men are what their mothers made them.
> RALPH WALDO EMERSON (1803–82)
> *Conduct of Life:* 'Fate'

> And say to mothers what a holy charge
> Is theirs – with what a kingly power their love
> Might rule the fountains of the new-born mind.
>> LYDIA HUNTLEY SIGOURNEY (1791–1865)
>> *The Mother of Washington*

I would desire for a friend the son who never resisted the tears of his mother.
> LACRETELLE

Behold, I was shapen in wickedness: and in sin hath my mother conceived me.

PSALMS 51:5

What is home without a mother?

ALICE HAWTHORNE (1827–1902)
title of poem

A ship under sail, a man in complete armour, and a woman with a big belly, are the three handsomest sights in the world.

JAMES HOWELL (1594–1666)
Proverbs

A man's mother is so tissued and woven into his life and brain that he can no more describe her than describe the air and sunlight that bless his days.

CHRISTOPHER MORLEY
Mince Pie: 'Our Mothers'

Cry, baby, cry,
Put your finger in your eye,
And tell your mother it wasn't I.

J.O. HALLIWELL
Nursery Rhymes
1853

God could not be everywhere and therefore he made mothers.

JEWISH PROVERB

So loving to my mother
That he might not beteem the winds of heaven
Visit her face too roughly.

WILLIAM SHAKESPEARE (1564–1616)
Hamlet

They say there is no other
Can take the place of mother.

GEORGE BERNARD SHAW (1856–1950)
The Admirable Bashville

Thus she spoke; and I longed to embrace my dead mother's ghost. Thrice I tried to clasp her image, and thrice it slipped through my hands, like a shadow, like a dream.

HOMER (c. 700 BC)
The Odyssey

Who is best taught? He who has first learned from his mother.

THE TALMUD

He maketh the barren woman to keep house: and to be a joyful mother of children.

> PSALMS 20:7

O little did my mother ken
The day she cradled me,
The lands I was to travel in
Or the death I was to die!

> THE QUEEN'S MARIES
> *The Oxford Book of Ballads*

Mary was that Mother mild.

> CECIL FRANCES ALEXANDER (1818–95)
> *Once in Royal David's City*
> 1848

A mother is a mother still,
The holiest thing alive.

> SAMUEL TAYLOR COLERIDGE (1772–1834)
> *The Three Graves*

I am yet so near the manners of my mother, that upon the least occasion more mine eyes will tell tales of me.

> WILLIAM SHAKESPEARE (1564–1616)
> *Twelfth Night*

A father may turn his back on his child, brothers and sisters may become inveterate enemies, husbands may desert their wives, wives their husbands. But a mother's love endures through all.

WASHINGTON IRVING (1783–1859)
The Sketch Book
1820

I cannot bear a mother's tears.

PUBLIUS VERGILIUS MARO VIRGIL (70–19 BC)
Aeniad

The mother may forget the child
That smiles sae sweetly on her knee;
But I'll remember thee, Glencairn,
And a' that thou hast done for me.

ROBERT BURNS (1759–96)
Lament for James, Earl of Glencairn

Mother of the Fair Delight,
Thou handmaid perfect in God's sight.

DANTE GABRIEL ROSSETTI (1828–82)
Ave

Mother of dead dogs.
> THOMAS CARLYLE (1795–1881)
> in a letter to John Carlyle, 11 September 1840
> from Froude's *Carlyle*, 1884

If I were hanged on the highest hill,
Mother o' mine, O mother o' mine!
I know whose love would follow me still,
Mother o' mine, O mother o' mine!
> RUDYARD KIPLING (1865–1936)
> *Mother o' Mine*

In the gruelling Indian heat and dazzling light, my mother, an unusually pretty girl of twenty-two or so, went around looking like some kind of wonderful half-butterfly, half-multi-coloured flower, with her swirling skirts of muslin figured with patterns of immense roses … Being in love, I was totally involved in every smallest detail of my mother's charisma.
> JULIA STRACHEY (1901–79)
> *Julia: A Portrait by Herself and Frances Partridge*
> 1983

Simply having children does not make mothers.
> JOHN A. SHEDD
> *Salt from my Attic*

I have said to corruption, Thou art my Father: to the Worm, Thou art my mother, and my sister.
>JOB 17:14

Children are the anchors that hold a mother to life.
>SOPHOCLES (495–406 BC)
>*Phaedra*

The future destiny of a child is always the work of the mother.
>NAPOLEON BONAPARTE (1769–1821)

Unhappy is the man for whom his own mother has not made all other mothers venerable.
>JEAN PAUL RICHTER (1763–1825)
>*Hesperus*
>1795

Nice while it lasted, an' now it is over –
Tear out your 'eart an' good-bye to your lover!
What's the use o' grievin, when the mother that
  bore you
(Mary, pity women!) knew it all before you?
>RUDYARD KIPLING (1865–1936)
>*Mary, Pity Women*

Mother and maiden
Was never none but she!
Well may such a lady
God's mother be.
   I Sing of a Maiden
   15th century carol, in *The Oxford Book of Carols*

Oliver's temperature zig-zagged across the chart, so that he could not be allowed home the next day.

'Really, Mrs Davenant!' said a stout and exasperated woman, who was the almoner, 'your child is not the only one in the hospital.'

'He is the only child of mine in the hospital,' said Julia.
   ELIZABETH TAYLOR (1912–75)
   At Mrs Lippincote's

An author who speaks about his own books is almost as bad as a mother who talks about her own children.
   BENJAMIN DISRAELI (1804–81)
   quoted in Meynell's *Disraeli*

She's somebody's mother, boys, you know,
For all she's aged and poor and slow.
   MARY DOW BRINE (*fl.* 1878)
   Somebody's Mother

Who ran to help me when I fell,
And would some pretty story tell,
Or kiss the place to make it well,
My mother.
>   ANN TAYLOR (1782–1866)
>   *My Mother*

My father argued sair – my mother didna speak,
But she look'd in my face till my heart was like to
    break.
>   LADY ANNE BARNARD (1750–1825)
>   *Auld Robin Gray*

My mother groan'd, my father wept,
Into the dangerous world I leapt;
Helpless, naked, piping loud,
Like a fiend hid in a cloud.
>   WILLIAM BLAKE (1757–1827)
>   *Songs of Experience*

And all my mother came into mine eyes
And gave me up to tears.
>   WILLIAM SHAKESPEARE (1564–1616)
>   *Hamlet*

Behold, I was shapen in wickedness: and in sin hath my Mother conceived me.

But lo, thou requirest truth in the inward parts: and shalt make me to understand wisdom secretly.

Thou shalt purge me with hyssop, and I shall be clean: thou shalt wash me, and I shall be whiter than snow.

Thou shalt make me hear of joy and gladness: that the bones which thou hast broken may rejoice.

PSALM 49
The Book of Common Prayer

The world has no such flowers in any land,
And no such pearl in any gulf the sea,
As any babe on any mother's knee.

ALGERNON CHARLES SWINBURNE (1837–1909)
Pelagius

As one whom his mother comforteth, so will I comfort you.

ISAIAH 46:13

I [Nature] am called a mother, but I am a grave.

ALFRED DE VIGNY (1797–1863)
La Maison du Berger
1864

Thou has never in thy life
Show'd thy dear mother any courtesy;
When she – poor hen! fond of no second brood –
Has cluck'd thee to the wars, and safely home,
Loaden with honour.
WILLIAM SHAKESPEARE (1564–1616)
Coriolanus

Far from the sun and summer-gale,
In thy green lap was Nature's darling laid,
What time, where lucid Avon stray'd,
To him the mighty Mother did unveil
Her aweful face: the dauntless child
Stretch'd forth his little arms, and smiled.
THOMAS GRAY (1716–71)
The Progress of Poesy

Thou art thy mother's glass, and she in thee
Calls back the lovely April of her prime.
WILLIAM SHAKESPEARE (1564–1616)
Sonnets

We'll 'elp 'im for 'is mother, an' 'e'll 'elp us by-an'-by!
RUDYARD KIPLING (1865–1936)
The Shut-Eye Sentry

All women become like their mothers. That is their tragedy. No man does. That's his.

OSCAR WILDE (1854–1900)
The Importance of Being Earnest

Children, look into those eyes, listen to the dear voice, notice the feeling of even a single touch that is bestowed upon you by that gentle hand! Make much of it while yet you have that most precious of all good gifts – a loving mother. Read the unfathomable love of those eyes, the kind anxiety of that tone and look, however slight your pain. In after life you may have friends, and dear friends, but never will you have again the inexpressible love and gentleness lavished upon you, which none but mother bestows.

THOMAS BABINGTON MACAULEY (1800–59)
Essays
1834

PARIS: Younger than she are happy mothers made.
CAPULET: And too soon marr'd are those so early made.

WILLIAM SHAKESPEARE (1564–1616)
Romeo and Juliet

Can you hear me, mother?
SANDY POWELL (1900–82)

Of Hayley's birth this was the happy lot:
His mother on his father him begot.
WILLIAM BLAKE (1757–1827)
On Friends and Foes

The boy [his son] is the most powerful of all the
Hellenes; for the Hellenes are commanded by the
Athenians, the Athenians by myself, myself by the
boy's mother, and the mother by her boy.
THEMISTOCLES (528–462 BC)
from Plutarch's *Lives*

This shall be thy lullaby
Rocking on the stormy sea,
Though it roar in thunder wild
Sleep, stilly sleep, my dark haired child.

When our shuddering boat was crossing
Elderno lake so rudely tossing
Then 'twas first my nursling smiled;
Sleep, softly sleep, my fair browed child.

41

Waves about thy cradle break,
Foamy tears are on thy cheek,
Yet the Ocean's self grows mild
When it bears my slumbering child.
> EMILY BRONTE (1818–48)
> *Song to A. A.*
> from *The Poems*, 1846

I was so young, I loved him so, I had
No mother, God forgot me, and I fell.
> ELIZABETH BARRETT BROWNING (1806–61)
> *A Blot in the 'Scutcheon*
> 1843

Don't tell my mother I'm living in sin,
Don't let the old folks know.
> A.P. HERBERT (1890–1971)
> *Laughing Ann*
> 1925

A mother who boasts two boys was ever accounted rich.
> ROBERT BROWNING (1812–89)
> *Ivan Ivanovitch*

Of all human struggles there is none so treacherous and remorseless as the struggle between the artist man and the mother woman.

> GEORGE BERNARD SHAW (1856–1950)
> *Man and Superman*
> 1903

Mother died today. Or perhaps it was yesterday. I don't know.

> ALBERT CAMUS (1913–60)
> *The Outsider*
> 1944

No matter how old a mother is she watches her middle-aged children for signs of improvement.

> FLORIDA SCOTT-MAXWELL
> *Measure of My Days*
> 1968

Memory, the mother of the Muses.

> PLATO (428–348 BC)
> *Dialogues*

For thee, O now a silent soul, my brother,
Take at my hands this garland and farewell.
Thin is the leaf, and chill the wintry smell,
And chill the solemn earth, a fatal mother,
With sadder than the Niobean womb
And in the hollow of her breasts a tomb.
> ALGERNON CHARLES SWINBURNE (1837–1909)
> *Ave atque Vale*

Mother knows best.
> EDNA FERBER (1887–1968)
> *Mother Knows Best*
> 1927

Mother may I go out to swim?
Yes my darling daughter.
Fold your clothes up neat and trim,
And don't go near the water.
> WALTER DE LA MARE (1873–1956)
> *The Scarecrow*
> 1945

A mother never realises that her children are no
longer children.
> HOLBROOK JACKSON (1874–1948)
> *All Manner of Folk*
> 1912

'My country, right or wrong', is a thing that no patriot would think of saying except in a desperate case. It is like saying, 'My mother, drunk or sober'.

G. K. CHESTERTON (1874–1936)
Defendant
1901

Women know
The way to rear up children (to be just),
They know the simple, merry, tender, knack
Of tying sashes, fitting baby-shoes,
And stringing pretty words that make no sense.

ELIZABETH BARRETT BROWNING (1806–61)
Aurora Leigh

My mother used to say, Delia, if s-e-x ever rears its ugly head, close your eyes before you see the rest of it.

ALAN AYCKBOURN (1939 –)
Bedroom Farce
1978

Few misfortunes can befall a boy which bring worse consequences than to have a really affectionate mother.

W. SOMERSET MAUGHAM (1874–1965)
Writer's Notebook
1947

If a writer has to rob his mother, he will not hesitate; the 'Ode on a Grecian Urn' is worth any number of old ladies.

> WILLIAM FAULKNER (1897–1962)
> quoted in the *Paris Review*,
> 1959

Lizzie Borden took an axe
And gave her mother forty whacks;
When she saw what she had done
She gave her father forty one!

> ANON
> *The Tale of Lizzie Borden*

Love droops, youth fades;
The leaves of friendship fall;
A mother's love outlives them all.

> OLIVER WENDELL HOLMES (1809–94)

Come to the bridal-chamber, Death!
Come to the mother's, when she feels,
For the first time, her first-born's breath.

> FITZ-GREENE HALLECK (1790–1867)
> *Marco Bozzaris*

The future of society is in the hands of mothers; if the world was lost through woman, she alone can save it.

LOUIS DE BEAUFORT

She was maintaining the prime truth of woman, the universal mother: that if a thing is worth doing, it is worth doing badly.

G.K. CHESTERTON (1874–1936)
What's Wrong with the World
1910

Parenthood: that state of being better chaperoned than you were before marriage.

MARCELINE COX
in *Ladies' Home Journal*
1944

The real menace in dealing with a five-year-old is that in no time at all you begin to sound like a five-year-old.

JEAN KERR
Please Don't Eat the Daisies
1957

The parting injuctions
Of mothers and wives
Are one of those functions
That poison their lives.
    CLARENCE DAY
    Scenes from Mesozoic

His mother, who was patient, being dead.
    COVENTRY PATMORE (1823–96)
    The Unknown Eros
    011877

Nobody can misunderstand a boy like his own mother.
    NORMAN DOUGLAS (1868–1952)

No woman can shake off her mother. There should be no mothers, only women.
    GEORGE BERNARD SHAW (1856–1950)
    Too Good to be True
    1934

A fingering slave,
One that would peep and botanize
Upon his mother's grave?
A reasoning, self-sufficing thing,
An intellectual All-in-all!
WILLIAM WORDSWORTH (1770–1850)
A Poet's Epitaph

I was still young enough then to be sleeping with my
Mother, which to me seemed life's whole purpose ...
Alone, at that time, of all the family, I was her
chosen dream companion chosen from all for her
extra love; my right, so it seemed to me.
LAURIE LEE (1914–)
Cider With Rosie
1959

Never allow your child to call you by your first name.
He hasn't known you long enough.
FRAN LEBOWITZ
Social Studies
1981

My mother loved children – she would have given
anything if I'd been one.
GROUCHO MARX (1895–1977)

It is pretty generally held that all a woman needs to do
to know all about children is to have some.
> HEYWOOD BROWN
> *Collected Edition*
> 1941

Mother, give me the sun.
> HENRIK IBSEN (1828–1906)
> *Ghosts*

My mother bids me bind my hair
With bands of rosy hue,
Tie up my sleeves with ribbons rare,
And lace my bodice blue.
> ANNE HUNTER (1742–1821)
> *My Mother Bids Me Bind my Hair*

My mother bids me bind my heir,
But not the trade where I should bind,
To place a boy – the how and where –
It is the plague of parent-kind!
> THOMAS HOOD (1799–1845)
> *My Son and Heir*

See yon pale stripling! When a boy,
A mother's pride, a father's joy.
SIR WALTER SCOTT (1771–1832)
Rokeby
1813

Blessed are the mothers of the Earth, for they have combined the practical and the spiritual into the workable way of human life.
WILLIAM L. STINGER

Her court was pure; her life serene;
God gave her peace; her land reposed;
A thousand claims to reverence closed
In her a Mother, wife and queen.
ALFRED, LORD TENNYSON (1809–92)
To the Queen
1851

He smiled and said, 'Sir, does your mother know that you are out?'
REVEREND R.H. BARHAM (1788–1845)
Misadventures at Margate

My mother had a good deal of trouble with me but I think she enjoyed it. She had none at all with my brother Henry, who was two years younger than I, and I think that the unbroken monotony of his goodness and truthfulness and obedience would have been a burden to her but for the relief and variety which I furnished in the other direction.

MARK TWAIN (1835–1910)
The Autobiography of Mark Twain
1924

Nature's loving proxy, the watchful mother.

EDWARD GEORGE BULWER-LYTTON (1803–73)
The Caxtons
1849

Mothers' darlings make but milksop heroes.

PROVERB

One race there is of men, one of gods, but from one mother we both draw our breath.

PINDAR (518–438 BC)
Nemean Odes

'Who was your mother?' 'Never had none!' said the child, with another grin. 'Never had any mother? What do you mean? Where were you born?' 'Never was born!' persisted Topsy.

> HARRIET BEECHER STOWE (1811–96)
> *Uncle Tom's Cabin*
> 1852

He cannot have god for his father who has not the church for his mother.

> ST CYPRIAN (*d.* 258 AD)
> *De Cath. Eccl. Unitate*

Begin, baby boy, to recognise your mother with a smile.

> PUBLIUS VERGILIUS MARO VIRGIL (70–19 BC)
> *Eclogue*

O wonderful son, that can so astonish a mother!

> WILLIAM SHAKESPEARE (1564–1616)
> *Hamlet*

So may'st thou live, till like ripe fruit thou drop
Into thy mother's lap.

> JOHN MILTON (1608–74)
> *Paradise Lost*
> 1663

Many men, my Lord,
Of hardihood sufficient, have been known
To hold the memories of their mothers dear.
  JOHN DAVIDSON (1857–1909)
  The Ordeal

To man the earth seems altogether
No more a mother, but a step-dame rather.
  DU BARTAS (1544–90)
  Divine Weeks and Works

Beer will grow 'mothery', and ladies fair
Will grow like beer.
  THOMAS HOOD (1799–1845)
  Stag-Eyed Lady

In the heavens above
The angels, whispering to one another,
Can find, amid their burning terms of love,
None so devotional as that of 'mother'.
  EDGAR ALLAN POE (1809–49)
  To My Mother

Is not a young mother one of the sweetest sights which life shows us?

> WILLIAM MAKEPEACE THACKERAY (1811–63)
> *The Newcomes*
> 1853

If there be aught surpassing human deed or word or thought it is a mother's love.

> MARCHIONESS DE SPADARA

What instruction the baby brings to the mother!

> T.W. HIGGINSON

Honoured Mother, I wish you write to Caperny Cray to send me my poney, and my books, and I wish that you would come and see me as soon as possible, and bring me some candied lemon, and figs, and cakes, and write to my Father to tell him to send home Sweet meats, for your dutyful son, Thomas Love Peacock.

> THOMAS LOVE PEACOCK (1785–1866)
> letter

Maternal love: a miraculous substance which God multiplies as He divides it.
VICTOR HUGO (1802–85)

I have not wept these forty years; but now my mother comes afresh into my eyes.
JOHN DRYDEN (1631–1700)

He that wipes the child's nose kisseth the mother's cheek.
GEORGE HERBERT (1593–1633)
Outlandish Proverbs
1640

Mother is the name for God in the lips and hearts of little children.
WILLIAM MAKEPEACE THACKERAY (1811–63)
Vanity Fair
1847

Despise not thy mother when she is old.
PROVERBS 23:22

They say that man is mighty,
He governs land and sea,
He wields a mighty sceptre
O'er lesser powers that be;
But a mightier power and stronger
Man from his throne has hurled,
And the hand that rocks the cradle
Is the hand that rules the world.
W.R. WALLACE (*d.* 1881)
What Rules the World?

Thou, while thy babes around thee cling,
Shalt show us how divine a thing
A woman may be made.
WILLIAM WORDSWORTH (1770–1850)
To a Young Lady

But one on earth is better than the wife; that is the mother.
LEOPOLD SCHEFER

One good mother is worth a hundred schoolmasters.
PROVERB

Lovers grow cold, men learn to hate their wives,
And only parents' love can last our lives.
ROBERT BROWNING (1812–89)
Pippa Passes

Mother, a maiden is a tender thing,
And best by her that bore her understood.
ALFRED, LORD TENNYSON (1809–89)
The Marriage of Geraint

O lovelier daughter of a lovely mother!
QUINTUS HORATIUS FLACCUS HORACE (65–8 BC)
Odes

I am not what I was in the reign of the good Cinata.
Forbear, cruel mother of sweet loves.
QUINTUS HORATIUS FLACCUS HORACE (65–8 BC)
Odes

Children suck the mother when they are young, and
the father when they are old.
JOHN RAY (1627–1705)
English Proverbs
1670

He that hath a wife and children hath given hostages
to fortune.
>   FRANCIS BACON (1561–1626)
>   *Of Marriage*

Children mothered by the street,
Blossoms of humanity,
Poor soiled blossoms in the dust,
In your features may be traced
Childhood's beauty half-effaced.
>   MATHILDE BLIND
>   *Sheet-Children's Dance*

The many-tattered,
Little, old-faced, peaking, sister-turned-mother.
>   ROBERT BROWNING (1812–89)
>   *Christmas Eve*

The bearing and training of a child
Is woman's wisdom.
>   ALFRED, LORD TENNYSON (1809–92)
>   *The Princess*

A mother's love, in a degree, sanctifies the most worthless offspring.

HOSEA BALLOU

A woman's love
Is mighty, but a mother's heart is weak,
And by its weakness overcomes.

JAMES RUSSELL LOWELL (1819–91)

The mother's love is at first an absorbing delight, blunting all other sensibilities; it is an expansion of the animal existence.

GEORGE ELIOT (1819–80)
The Mill on the Floss
1860

Mother calls me Willie, but the fellers call me Bill!

EUGENE FIELD (1850–95)
Jest 'Fore Christmas

The child takes most of his nature of the mother, besides speech, manners, and inclination.

HERBERT SPENCER (1820–1903)
Essays on Education
1861

65

Mothers, wives and maids,
Those be the fools wherewith priests manage men.
 ROBERT BROWNING (1812–89)
 The Ring and the Book

Every girl ought to have her mother's religion, and
every wife her husband's.
 JEAN-JACQUES ROUSSEAU (1712–78)
 Emile
 1762

I will go back to the great sweet mother,
Mother and lover of men, the sea.
I will go down to her, I and no other,
Close with her, kiss her and mix her with me.
 ALGERNON CHARLES SWINBURNE (1837–1909)
 The Triumph of Time

My mother was dead for five years before I knew that I
had loved her very much.
 LILLIAN HELLMAN
 An Unfinished Woman

As well as her love for her child then, there exists in every mother an aversion for the child ... If you recognise mother love, do you also recognise mother hate?

GEORG GRODDECK
The Book of the It

A man who has been the indisputable favourite of his mother keeps for life the feeling of a conqueror, that confidence of success that often induces real success.

SIGMUND FREUD (1856–1939)
The Letters of Sigmund Freud

O mother Ida, many-fountained Ida,
Dear mother Ida, hearken ere I die.

ALFRED, LORD TENNYSON (1809–92)
Oenone
1832

Nobody can have the soul of me. My mother has had it, and nobody can have it again. Nobody can come into my very self again, and breathe me like an atmosphere.

D.H. LAWRENCE (1885–1930)
Selected Letters

My Dear Mother

You will think that I entirely forgot you, but I assure you that you are greatly mistaken, I think of you always and often sigh to think of the distance between us two loving creatures of nature.

> MARJORY FLEMING (1803–11)
> letter to her mother in the year she died, aged 8
> from *The Story of Pet Marjorie* by L. McBean, 1904

Let France have good mothers and she will have good sons.

> NAPOLEON BONAPARTE (1769–1821)

The mother cult is something that will set future generations roaring with laughter.

> GUSTAVE FLAUBERT (1821–80)
> *Letters of Gustave Flaubert*

Maids must be wives and mothers, to fulfil
Th' entire and holiest end of woman's being.

> FRANCES ANNE KEMBLE (1809–93)
> *Woman's Heart*

It is not that women have less impulse than men to be creative and productive. But through the ages having children, for women who wanted children, has been so satisfying that it has taken some special circumstances – spinsterhood, barrenness or widowhood – to let women give their whole minds to other work.

> MARGARET MEAD
> *Blackberry Winter*

When her mother tends her before the laughing
    mirror,
Tying up her laces, looping up her hair.
> GEORGE MEREDITH (1828–1909)
> *Love in the Valley*

No one but doctors and mothers know what it means to have interruptions.

> KARL A. MENNINGER
> *The Human Mind*

Evening star, you bring all things which the bright dawn has scattered: you bring the sheep, you bring the goat, you bring the child back to its mother.

> SAPPHO (*c.* 612 BC)
> *Fragment, 120*

It is not as thy mother says, but as thy neighbours say.
T. FULLER
Gnomologia: Adagies and Proverbs
1732

Women are aristocrats, and it is always the mother who makes us feel that we belong to the better sort.
JOHN LANCASTER SPALDING
Things of the Mind

One day, Mamma said: 'Conrad dear,
I must go out and leave you here.
But mind now, Conrad, what I say,
Don't suck your thumb while I'm away.
The great tall tailor always comes
To little boys that suck their thumbs,
And ere they dream what he's about,
He takes his great sharp scissors out
And cuts their thumbs clean off – and then,
You know, they never grow again.'
HEINRICH HOFFMANN (1809–74)
The Story of Little Suck-a-Thumb
in *Struwwelpeter,*
1845

Who has not watched a mother stroke her child's cheek or kiss her child in a certain way and felt a nervous shudder at the possessive outrage done to a free solitary human soul?

    JOHN COWPER POWYS (1872–1963)
    The Meaning of Culture

So shut your eyes while mother sings
Of wonderful sights that be,
And you shall see the beautiful things
As you rock on the misty sea
Where the old shoe rocked the fishermen three
  Wynken,
  Blynken,
  And Nod.
  EUGENE FIELD (1850–95)
  Dutch Lullaby

Everybody knows that a good mother gives her children a feeling of trust and stability. She is their earth. She is the one they can count on for the things that matter most of all. She is their food and their bed and the extra blanket when it grows cold in the night; she is their warmth and their health and their shelter; she is the one they want to be near when they cry.

    KATHERINE BUTLER HATHAWAY
    The Journals and Letters of the Little Locksmith

In the eyes of its mother every beetle is a gazelle.
MOROCCAN PROVERB

Mothers, at least American mothers, are a weird lot. Some sea-change seems to happen in a woman as soon as she becomes a mother ... All sorts of virtues claim her, and she claims them.
JAMES JONES
World War Two

The good old dominion, the blessed mother of us all.
THOMAS JEFFERSON (1743–1826)
his last words

I never had a mother. I suppose a mother is one to whom you hurry when you are troubled.
EMILY DICKINSON (1830–86)
Letters of Emily Dickinson

Mother was the absolutely dominating force in all our lives. Even her mere existence in those last years, was a sort of centre around which we revolved, in thought if not in our actual movements. We shall be living henceforth in an essentially different world.
GEORGE SANTAYANA (1863–1952)
Letters of George Santayana

When the hounds of spring are on winter's traces,
The mother of months in meadow or plain
Fills the shadows and windy places
With lisp of leaves and ripple of rain.
>   ALGERNON CHARLES SWINBURNE (1837–1909)
>   *Atalanta in Calydon*
>   1865

And doubtful joys the father move,
And tears are on the mother's face,
As parting with a long embrace
She enters other realms of love.
>   ALFRED, LORD TENNYSON (1809–92)
>   *In Memoriam*
>   1850

Very, very early in my boyhood I had acquired the
habit of going about alone to amuse myself in my own
way, and it was only after years, when my age was
about twelve, that my mother told me how anxious
this singularity used to make her. She would miss me
when looking out to see what the children were
doing, and I would be called and searched for, to be
found hidden away somewhere in the plantation.
Then she began to keep an eye on me, and when I was
observed stealing off she would secretly follow and

watch me, standing motionless among the tall weeds or under the trees by the half-hour, staring at vacancy. This distressed her very much; then to her great relief and joy she discovered that there was a motive which she could understand and appreciate: that I was watching some living thing, an insect perhaps, but oftener a bird ... And as she loved all living things herself she was quite satisfied that I was not going queer in my head, for that was what she had been fearing.

> W.H. HUDSON (1841–1922)
> *Far Away and Long Ago: A Childhood in Argentina*
> 1918

The mother's heart is the child's schoolroom.

> HENRY WARD BEECHER (1813–87)
> *Proverbs from a Plymouth Pulpit*

My mother was accursed the night she bore me, and I am faint with envy of all the dead.

> EURIPIDES (485–404 BC)
> *Alcestis*

I did not throw myself into the struggle for life: I threw my mother into it.

> GEORGE BERNARD SHAW (1856–1950)
> *The Irrational Heart*

Margaret had wanted a girl, by way of variety, and was disappointed in the birth of a son. But with her usual felicity – without a thought of what the consequences might be – she soon tumbled to the idea that, if she allowed his hair to grow long and dressed him as a girl, she could satisfy her ambition; provided she never looked too closely at him in the bath.

RICHARD STRACHEY
A Strachey Child
1979

I miss thee, my mother! thy image is still
The deepest impress'd on my heart,
And the tablet so faithful in death must be chill,
Ere a line of that image depart.

ELIZA COOK (1818–89)
Poems
1870

A mother should give her children a superabundance of enthusiasm, that after they have lost all they are sure to lose on mixing with the world, enough may still remain to prompt and support them through great actions.

JULIUS CHARLES HARE (1795–1855
Guesses at Truth
1827

At length abandon your mother.
QUINTUS HORATIUS FLACCUS HORACE (65–8 BC)
Odes

O! men with sisters dear,
O! men with mothers and wives!
It is not linen you're wearing out
But human creatures' lives!
THOMAS HOOD (1799–1845)
The Song of the Shirt

The tie which links mother and child is of such pure and immaculate strength as to be never violated, except by those whose feelings are withered by vitiated society. Holy, simple, and beautiful in its construction, it is the emblem of all we can imagine of fidelity and truth.
WASHINGTON IRVING (1783–1859)
The Sketch Book
1820

Ask the mother if the child be like his father.
T. FULLER
Gnomologia: Adagies and Proverbs
1732

Would, Mother, thou couldst hear me tell
How oft, amid my brief career,
For sins and follies loud too well,
Hath fallen the free, repentant tear.
And, in the waywardness of youth,
How better thoughts have given to me
Contempt for error, love for truth,
'Mid sweet remembrances of thee.
JAMES ALDRICH

A diligent mother, a lazy daughter.
PORTUGUESE PROVERB

Thou wilt scarce be a man before thy mother.
JOHN FLETCHER (1579–1625)
Love's Cure
1623

A timid man's mother does not weep.
PROVERBS
Vulgate Bible

A pitiful mother makes a scald head.
GEORGE HERBERT (1593–1633)
Outlandish Proverbs
1640

How gladly would I meet
Mortality, my sentence, and be earth
Insensible! how glad would lay me down,
As in my mother's lap! There I should rest,
And sleep secure.
JOHN MILTON (1608–74)
Paradise Lost
1663

If Caesar had stabbed their mothers, they would have done no less.
WILLIAM SHAKESPEARE (1564–1616)
Julius Caesar

So to be loved, so to be wooed,
Oh, more than mortal woman should!
What if she fail or fall behind?
Lord, make me worthy, keep them blind!
KATHARINE TYNAN (1861–1931)
The Mother

Do you expect, forsooth, that a mother will hand down to her children principles which are upright and different from those which she herself has?
JUVENAL (*c.* 60 – *c.* 130 AD)
Satires

I have no pain, dear Mother, now;
But oh! I am so dry:
Just moisten poor Jim's lips once more;
And Mother, do not cry!
  EDWARD FARMER (1809–76)
  The Collier's Dying Child

The mother, wi' her needle an' her shears
Gars auld claes look amaist as weel's the new.
  ROBERT BURNS (1759–96)
  The Cotter's Saturday Night
  1785

He's all the mother's from the top to toe.
WILLIAM SHAKESPEARE (1564–1616)
Richard III

With proud thanksgiving, a mother for her
children,
England mourns for her dead across the sea.
ROBERT LAURENCE BINYON (1869–1943)
For the Fallen

If the mother had not been in the oven, she had never
sought her daughter there.
PROVERB

Here's to the happiest days of my life,
Spent in the arms of another man's wife –
My mother's.
TRADITIONAL TOAST

No mother's care
Shielded my infant innocence with prayer.
RICHARD SAVAGE (1698–1743)
The Bastard
1728

With more fortitude does a mother long for one out of many, than she who weeping cries, 'Thou wast my only one'.

    OVID (43BC–AD 17)

Mother, thou sole and only, thou not these,
Keep me in mind a little when I die,
Because I was thy first-born ...
I thought to live and make thee honourable.

    ALGERNON CHARLES SWINBURNE (1837–1909)
    Atalanta in Calydon
    1865

I recollect a nurse called Ann,
Who carried me about the grass,
And one fine day a fair young man
Came up and kissed the pretty lass:
She did not make the least objection!
Thinks I, Aha!
When I can talk I'll tell Mamma!
– And that's my earliest recollection.

    FREDERICK LOCKER-LAMPSON (1821–95)
    A Terrible Infant

The instruction received at the mother's knee, and the paternal lessons, together with the pious and sweet souvenirs of the fireside, are never effaced entirely from the soul.

ABBÉ FÉLICITÉ ROBERT DE LAMENNAIS (1782–1854)

The tenderness you have for your children is sufficient to enforce you to the utmost regard for the preservation of a life so necessary to their well-being.

LADY MARY WORTLEY MONTAGU (1689–1762)
letter to her daughter, the Countess of Bute
in *The Letters of Lady Mary Wortley Montagu*,
1837

Virtue and happiness are mother and daughter.

H.G. BOHN (1796–1884)
A Handbook of Proverbs
1855

Wild air, world-mothering air,
Nestling me everywhere.

GERARD MANLEY HOPKINS (1844–89)
The Blessed Virgin Compared to the Air We Breathe

87

Come little babe, come silly soul,
Thy father's shame, thy mother's grief,
Born as I doubt to all our dole,
And to thy self unhappy chief:
    Sing lullaby and lap it warm,
    Poor soul that thinks no creature harm.
    NICHOLAS BRETON (1545–1626)
    A Sweet Lullaby

There was standing the sorrowing Mother, beside the
cross weeping while her Son hung upon it.
    JACOPHONE DA TODI (1230–1306)
    Stabat Mater dolorosa

In the dark womb where I began
My mother's life made me a man.
Through all the months of human birth
Her beauty fed my common earth.
I cannot see, nor breathe, not stir,
But through the death of some of her.
    JOHN MASEFIELD (1878–1967)
    C.L.M.

Every woman is at heart a mother.
    EDWARD VERRALL LUCAS
    English essayist

Mother, a maiden is a tender thing,
And best by her that bore her understood.
ALFRED, LORD TENNYSON (1809–92)
Marriage of Geraint

He was not all a father's heart could wish;
But oh, he was my son – my only son.
My child.
JOANNA BAILLIE (1762–1851)
Orrae

While thy wife's mother lives, expect no peace.
WILLIAM GIFFORD (1756–1826)
Juvenal

The foot at the cradle and the hand at the reel
is a sign that a woman means to do weel.
SCOTTISH PROVERB

Standing with reluctant feet
Where the brook and river meet,
Womanhood and childhood fleet.
HENRY WADSWORTH LONGFELLOW (1807–1850)
Maidenhood

Thou, while they babes around thee cling,
Shalt show us how divine a thing
A woman may be made.
WILLIAM WORDSWORTH (1770–1850)
To a Young Lady

There is nothing more charming than to see a mother
with a child in her arms, and nothing more venerable
than a mother among a number of her children.
JOHANN WOLFGAG VON GOETHE (1749–1832)

A mother alone knows what it is to love and be
happy.
CHAMISSO

Oh, the love of a mother, love no one forgets;
miraculous bread which God distributes and multiplies; bread always spread by the paternal hearth,
whereat each has his portion, and all have it entire!
VICTOR HUGO (1802–85)

No mother worthy of the name ever gave herself
thoroughly for her child who did not feel that, after
all, she reaped what she had sown.
BEECHER

The mother's yearning feels the presence of the cherished child even in the degraded man.
>GEORGE ELIOT (1819–80)

A kiss from my mother made me a painter.
>BENJAMIN WEST

>While men sleep,
>Sad-hearted mothers leave that wakeful lie,
>To muse upon some darling child
>Roaming in youth's uncertain wild.
>>JOHN KEBLE 1792–1866)

The pleasing punishment that women bear.
>WILLIAM SHAKESPEARE (1564–1616)
>*The Comedy of Errors*

He's all the mother's, from the top to toe.
>WILLIAM SHAKESPEARE (1564–1616)
>*Richard III*

If the world were put into one scale and my mother into the other, the world would kick the beam.
>LORD LANGDALE

'What is wanting,' said Napoleon one day to Madame Campar, 'in order that the youth of France be well educated?'

'Good mothers,' was the reply.

The Emperor was most forcibly struck with this answer.

'Here,' said he, 'is a system in one word.'

ABBOTT

Where there is a mother in the house, matters speed well.

A.B. ALCOTT

And he who gives a child a treat
makes joy-bells ring in Heaven's street,
And he who gives a child a home
Builds palaces in kingdom come,
And she who gives a baby birth
Brings Saviour Christ again to Earth.

JOHN MASEFIELD (1878–1967)
The Everlasting Mercy
1911

In Rama was there a voice heard, lamentation, and weeping, and great mourning, Rachel weeping for her children, and would not be comforted, because they are not.

ST MATTHEW, 2:18